The 110 Precepts

That Guided Our

First President

In War and Peace

Rules of Civility

Edited and with commentary by

Richard Brookhiser

The Free Press
New York • London • Toronto • Sydney • Singapore

THE FREE PRESS
A Division of Simon & Schuster Inc.
1230 Avenue of the Americas
New York, NY 10020

Copyright © 1997 by Richard Brookhiser

All rights reserved, including the right of reproduction
in whole or in part in any form.

The Free Press and colophon are trademarks of Simon & Schuster Inc.

Designed by Kim Llewellyn

Manufactured in the United States of America

10 9 8 7 6 5 4 3 2 1

Library of Congress Cataloging-in-Publication Data is available

ISBN 0-684-83723-4

For Esther Safer

Introduction

How do you become a great man? Two and a half centuries ago, a teenage boy in Virginia took his first steps by copying 110 rules into a notebook. George Washington went on to become a very great man indeed—easily the most successful revolutionary leader of modern times. (It's easier to win revolutions, we've discovered, than to run countries. Washington excelled at both.) He was shaped by many forces, from battles to books. But one of the earliest, and most important, was "The Rules of Civility & Decent Behavior in Company and Conversation." Modern Americans can still profit from his—and its—example.

When Washington had been president for seven years, a foreign diplomat's wife observed that he had "perfect good breeding, & a correct knowledge of even the etiquette of a court," though how he had acquired it, "heaven knows." The way he acquired it was by taking good advice early in life. Eighteenth-century Americans were eager for good advice, especially advice concerning their conduct. Children who wanted to be more grown up, and adults who wanted to be smarter, shrewder, or more couth, consumed manuals of advice and instruction, written here or abroad.

The all-American dispenser of good advice was Washington's partner in revolution, Benjamin Franklin, in his *Poor Richard's Almanac* ("God helps them that help themselves," "Have you somewhat to do tomorrow, do it today") and his *Autobiography* ("Eat not to dullness; drink not to elevation," "Resolve to perform what you ought; perform without fail what you resolve"). Franklin's maxims in time spread throughout the English-speaking world. D. H. Lawrence remembered them from a "scrubby little almanac" of his father's—and wished he didn't. "Probably I haven't gotten over those Poor Richard tags yet. I rankle still with them."

People want advice on their behavior when they are rising in the world. Even as America's relatively open society gave people a chance to better themselves, it made them anxious about how much better they had actually become. Early Americans, who were almost all WASPs, also had a religious history of self-examination—what one historian called the "iron couch of introspection." So they turned to books of advice.

Was all the busy advice giving and taking worth it? In one of his pieces of journalism, Franklin wryly suggests that the exertions of his fellow countrymen were wasted. He describes a crowd gathered for a sale, who ask an old man to tell them how they should live when times are hard. The old man gives them a fistful of maxims about frugality and temperance, drawn from Poor Richard. "Thus the old gentleman ended his harangue. The people heard it, and approved the doctrine, and immediately practiced the contrary, just as if it had been a common sermon; for the [sale] opened, and they began to buy extravagantly, notwithstanding all his cautions. . . ." But, years later, Franklin gave a more hopeful judgment. ". . . on the whole, though I never arrived at the perfection I had been so ambitious of obtaining, but fell far short of it, yet I was, by the endeavor, a better and a happier man than I otherwise should have been had I not attempted it."

Young Washington came by his rules in a roundabout

way. They were first compiled by French Jesuits in 1595, in a set of maxims called *Bienséance de la Conversation entre les Hommes* (Decency of Conversation among Men). The Jesuits, besides being missionaries, scholars, and all-purpose shock troops of the Pope, specialized in educating the children of the powerful. A guide to gentlemanly behavior would provide a popular service, and the Jesuits' rules were translated into Latin and several modern European languages.

In 1640, they appeared in English as *Youths Behavior, or Decency in Conversation amongst Men.* The translator was listed as Francis Hawkins, a twelve-year-old boy, who had supposedly done the work when he was eight. (The rules of civility of book publishing, then as now, tolerated a considerable degree of exaggeration.) Whoever translated them, the rules proved to be popular, going through eleven printings by 1672, with various extensions and supplements, including a "Decency in Conversation amongst Women." This last, added by a Puritan printer, shows that good breeding was interesting to both sexes, and all religions.

How they got to Virginia and George Washington is a mystery. A nineteenth-century historian, Moncure D.

Conway, who first discovered the Jesuit origin of the rules, believed they came to George directly from the French, skipping over Hawkins entirely. Washington never learned French, but Conway learned of a French Protestant minister who had lived near Fredericksburg, Virginia, just across the Rappahannock from Ferry Farm, the home of George's mother, and who could have translated them for his young neighbor. Later scholars have concluded that Washington's rules, though they are shortened and modernized versions of Hawkins, follow him closely. So they dismiss the Frenchman as an intermediary, and assume that someone—perhaps a tutor or a schoolteacher, perhaps George's father or one of his older half brothers—put a later version of the set in his hands and told him to write them out.

Youths Behavior was divided into seven sections, and "The Rules of Civility" follows the categories: General and mixt Precepts (rules 1–24); First Duties & Ceremonies in Conversation (rules 25–36); Of the fashions of qualifying or titleing of persons (rules 37–50); Of Clothes & Arraying the Body (rules 51 and 52); Of walking, be it alone, or in Company (rules 53–57); Of Discourse (rules 58–89); Of Carriage at the table (rules

90–107). The last three rules come from an appendix.

What is evident from reading these categories, or from even a casual dip into the Rules, is how few of them seem to deal with morals. Rule #108 rewords the Fifth Commandment ("Honor & obey your natural parents although they be poor") and offers a pale reflection of the First ("When you speak of God or His attributes, let it be seriously & with reverence"). Rule #109 is the only rule to mention sin ("Let your recreations be manful not sinful"—a veiled warning against whoring?). Rule #110 is a serious thought—"Labor to keep alive in your breast that little spark of celestial fire called conscience"—but it is so brief, and so long in coming, that Washington's biographers can't decide whether it is the crown of the whole, or a throwaway. The overwhelming majority of the rules deal with etiquette.

Etiquette was an important matter in the eighteenth century. One of the first orders of business of Congress under the Constitution was to decide what George Washington should be called. The House of Representatives wanted what eventually became his title, and the title of all his successors—"The President of the United States"—but the Senate vainly held out for something

Commemoration
of the Battle of Trenton

more elaborate, such as "His Highness the President of the United States and Protector of the Rights of the Same" (even "fire companies" and "cricket club[s]," one Senator complained, had plain presidents). Nowadays, when presidents are seen in jogging shorts, and even tell us about their underwear, and many Americans are much more informal than that, such concerns seem quaint. What use is etiquette in an age of daytime television and drive-time radio?

Many of the rules are time-bound. Some prescribe ways of coping with life in an era that was more coarse. When even a trip as short as New York City to Albany was a three-day expedition, and inns (where they existed) might put several guests in the same bed, people had to know not to spit into the fire (rule #9) or not to crush ticks in the presence of strangers (rule #13). Even as our hygiene and our housing have advanced, our social hierarchies have grown simpler. Rule #26 begins by discussing how to bow and doff your hat "to persons of distinction," such "as noblemen. . . ." In modern America there are no noblemen; hardly any hats (apart from baseball caps, which nobody doffs); and no one bows. Life in Washington's days could also

be crueler than it is now. "When you see a crime punished . . ." begins rule #23—not a rare event when people were put in the stocks, or hung on public gallows.
Our material conveniences, our social structure, and our
sensitive temperaments spare us from thinking about a
number of the issues raised in "The Rules of Civility."

But to dismiss "The Rules of Civility" as "mere" etiquette, and outdated etiquette at that, is to miss the
point. The rules address moral issues, but they address
them indirectly. To say that they focus on etiquette is
another way of saying that they are morally indirect.
This is what separates them from Franklin's maxims (as
well as the self-help and how-to manuals of today).
Franklin's little sermonettes are sometimes symbolic
("An empty bag cannot stand upright"), sometimes sar-
castic ("When there's marriage without love, there will
be love without marriage"). But they all make clear and
fairly blunt moral points. Don't waste time; don't get
drunk; don't tolerate poverty, if you value your indepen-
dence; don't accept coldness in marriage, if you value
fidelity. Some people profit from exhortation, as Franklin
felt he himself had, up to a point; some people—like his
shoppers, or D. H. Lawrence—don't.

"The Rules of Civility" take a different tack. They seek to form the inner man (or boy) by shaping the outer. They start with hats and posture and table manners, and work inward. The key is set in rule #1: "Every action done in company ought to be done with some sign of respect to those that are present." The effect of all the rules taken together is to remind you that you should not just do whatever feels right, or the first thing that comes into your head; rather, you should always be mindful of other people, and remember that they have sensibilities, and feelings of self-respect, that deserve your respect.

". . . [I]f you see any filth or thick spittle . . . upon the clothes of your companions," says rule #13, "put it off privately. . . ." In other words, don't make a fuss about helping someone. It only calls attention to his problem (and, incidentally, calls too much attention to your helpfulness). "Undertake not to teach your equal in the art himself professes; it savours of arrogancy" (rule #41). It savors of arrogance, because it is arrogance. Besides, your equal might be able to teach you something. "It's unbecoming to stoop much to one's meat" (rule #96). People don't like to sit next to someone hunched over his plate, paying more attention to his appetite than his companions. Thinking about sitting up straight also provides an automatic brake on gluttony. Sometimes the rules frankly counsel insincerity. Rule #23, about punished criminals, goes on to say that though "you may be inwardly pleased" by the spectacle of justice done, "shew pity to the offending sufferer." In extremis, even the sensibilities of a criminal are worth a little dissimulation. If this is hypocrisy, then, as Patrick Henry said of treason, make the most of it.

This awareness of the human environment—the sense that we navigate life through crowds of people who are, for all their differences of class or character, like ourselves—is what gives the rules their moral dimension, and their moral effect. "Attention must be paid!" declares Willy Loman's wife in *Death of a Salesman*. The way you get people to pay attention, say "The Rules of Civility," is by starting them off paying attention to their hats.

"The Rules of Civility" were an important help to Washington in his public life. He was genial by nature, enjoying company and a good joke; he got along well with men, and women. Washington's rules included no advice specifically addressed to conversation with women, but he somehow acquired the knack. "Fiction is to be sure the very life and soul of poetry," he wrote a lady poet who had sent him verses in praise of him. "To oblige you to make such an excellent poem on such a subject, without any materials but those of simple reality, would be as cruel as the edict of Pharaoh which compelled the children of Israel to manufacture bricks without the necessary ingredients." "[He] has so happy a faculty of appearing to accommodate and yet carrying his point," wrote Abigail Adams, evidently impressed with him. "that if he was really not one of the best-intentioned men in the world, he might be a very dangerous one."

But Washington also had a tremendous temper. This was a lifelong problem. When he was sixteen, a rich neighbor who was employing him as a surveyor wrote George's mother: "I wish I could say that he governs his temper." When Washington was sixty-one, Thomas Jefferson recorded a cabinet meeting at which President Washington "got into one of those passions when he cannot command himself." "Had he been born in the forests," wrote the painter Gilbert Stuart, who had the

Monmouth Courthouse—
the Commander in Chief
loses his temper with General Lee

opportunity to study Washington carefully while he sat for his portrait, "he would have been the fiercest man among the savage tribes."

Washington had a lot to be angry about over the course of his career: untrained soldiers, incompetent officers, difficult allies, quarrelsome associates (including Jefferson)—to say nothing of his own mistakes, from losing battles to misjudging people: Washington trusted Benedict Arnold—a man of great apparent civility, though little real decency—up to the moment he ran off to the enemy. But if he had gone into uncontrollable rages at every disappointment or disaster, he would have ruined his health, besides ruining his effectiveness as a leader.

Washington got some help reining in his temper from the Stoic example of the ancient Romans (the philosopher Seneca, whom he read as a teenager, wrote a whole essay on anger, and what a bad thing it was). But the earliest lessons came from the Rules. ". . . in reproving shew no sign of choler" (rule #45). "Speak not injurious words neither in jest nor earnest" (rule #65). "When you deliver a matter do it without passion . . ." (rule #83). "Be not angry at table whatever happens & if

George Washington

you have reason to be so, show it not but [put] on a cheerful countenance" (rule #105—that saving insincerity again).

The measure of Washington's success, despite his lapses, is that we have forgotten that he had a problem. We look at Stuart's glacial image, and a dozen other composed and almost emotionless portraits, from the face on Mount Rushmore to the bust on the quarter, and we assume that that's just the way Washington was. His contemporaries knew better; they saw the composure as an end product, the result of early training and continuous effort. The training, and the disposition to make the effort, came from the Rules.

The trajectory of Washington's life demanded that he be well mannered. He was the third son of a Virginia planter who was prosperous and ambitious, but not yet at the top of the social pyramid in his colony. Then Washington's father died when he was eleven. Obscurity beckoned, but rich in-laws gave the teenager an entrée into a more sophisticated world, and into military life. He needed some measure of polish in order to retain this first foothold. Despite several slips, he kept it, and climbed higher in Virginia society (marriage to Martha

*George Washington
marries Martha Custis, 1759*

Custis, a rich young widow, helped). In his forties des-
tiny beckoned, and from the time he became commander
of the Continental army, in 1775, until his death twenty-
four years later, his contacts were national and interna-
tional. Washington dealt with Indians, both allies and
potential enemies; with blacks, both slaves and freemen;
with Roman Catholics and Jews; with pacifist Quakers
and hell-raising Scotch-Irish frontiersmen; with Yankee
traders and Southern aristocrats; with generals
(American, French, and British) and privates; with ador-
ing crowds of strangers and with congressmen who,
however much they professed to admire him, might not
be disposed to give him what he wanted. Sometimes, the
only way to deal with some of these characters was to
be stern, to be cold, or (in the rarest of cases) to let slip
the leash on his rage. But up to the point of no return,
Washington was best served by civility. Politeness is the
first form of politics, and Washington had the most tax-
ing political task of anyone in his generation. He was
fortunate that, by the time he had assumed his greatest
responsibilities, civility had become second nature to him.
Rule #1 begins: "Every action done in company . . ."
Beginning in his forties, the company Washington kept

expanded from a plantation aristocracy to a continental republic. Decent behavior helped him lead it.

Not everybody in the founding generation agreed with Washington's notions of civility or civil society. The American Revolution produced no dictators, but there were several figures who might have auditioned for the role, had circumstances been different. Aaron Burr (who served under Washington in the war) once told Alexander Hamilton (who served on Washington's staff, and later in his administration) that "great spirits care little for petty morals." Burr, who later killed Hamilton in a duel and was prosecuted for treason, did not care about large morals either. The large ones depend on practicing, and understanding, the petty ones.

Washington went on to fame. Not so his Rules. They slumbered in their notebook until the early nineteenth century, when the historian Jared Sparks published fifty of them. The editions that have followed at intervals have been either biographical—satisfying our curiosity about the details of a famous man's life, even as we read books and articles about Washington's foxhounds, or his chinaware—or antiquarian: a quaint look at Ye Olde Times, a Williamsburg restoration of table manners.

Biography makes the Rules interesting, but too particular to Washington—no more useful to us than his dentures. Antiquarianism makes the Rules charming, but remote.

Americans still peruse vast quantities of advice and self-help literature. But until very recently, rules of civility were not among them. The abeyance of civility was due in part to the cult of authenticity, which has old American roots of its own, going back to Emerson and Thoreau. The sixties, and their wholesale successor the seventies, made authenticity a national orthodoxy. Even as fashions in authenticity changed, civility remained at a discount. Whether you grew your hair out like Jim Morrison, or buzzed it and dyed it like Dennis Rodman, you were not doing it as a sign of respect for others. "Play not the peacock, looking every where about you, to see if you be well deck't . . ." (Rule #54).

In part, the seeming irrelevance of civility nowadays is due to (or is rationalized by) our disgust with the century we live in. After the Holocaust and the gulag, when civilization itself can seem beside the point, what is the value of "Decent Behavior in Company and Conversation"?

The best answer to the second objection is a little history. Three months after the Senate and the House finished wrangling about George Washington's title, the French Revolution began. In its early stages, thousands of priests, women, children, and simple peasants were herded onto barges and drowned, and the former Queen was publicly humiliated and decapitated. Americans then did not know as much as we know about the drownings, but they certainly knew about the Queen: the revolutionaries killed her in public, because they were proud of killing her. This wasn't Auschwitz, but it partook of the same spirit. Our Age of Innocence overlapped with the dawn of the Age of Experience. Yet no one—certainly not Washington—felt released by the turmoil in France from the obligations of civility in Philadelphia, or Mount Vernon.

As for the cult of authenticity, one of the arguments against it is that in extreme cases it can encourage monsters. (Surely Hitler could have used more repression in his life, not less.) But it is not necessary to drag in the Third Reich in order to impeach authenticity's excesses. When everybody does his thing, a lot of nasty things get done, even in a society as decent and a regime as mild as ours. From the White House to the trailer parks, Americans act like boors and dress like louts because they are, in fact, boorish and loutish.

Another problem with authenticity is that it is so easily faked. The sincerity of self-helpers, empathic politicians, anguished rock artists, or preachers at megachurches may be real. But it may not. An actor can do wonders with a catch in his voice. Psychopaths, who spontaneously simulate the emotions others want of them, don't even have to act consciously. A man who tips his hat may harbor all manner of unpleasant thoughts, including indifference. But he has tipped his hat. Maybe the gesture, repeated often enough, will work inward, and stimulate a more magnanimous disposition.

There is a special reason why Washington's "Rules of Civility" are not taken seriously today—and that is the withering of the ambition to be great, and of the belief that greatness is possible. Twentieth-century Americans believe they can be rich, or powerful, or famous: we can found software empires in the garage, or become president, or cut demos that go platinum. If those achievements are beyond reach, we can be happy. Certainly we pursue happiness, as the therapies and workouts and self-help books attest. But greatness has vanished from the map of our minds.

It was there two hundred and fifty years ago, though, in a cluster of colonies that consisted of a handful of towns, a Third World economy, and millions of acres of trees. Even so, the backwoods lawyers and the seaport philosophers and the farmers with libraries thought they knew something about virtue and liberty, and they believed they could establish them in the world, if they made themselves fit for the task. In the same exercise book that contains "The Rules of Civility," there is a geography lesson which describes California as an island. George Washington did not know what California was, but he knew there were great things to be done in his country, and for it. The first step he took toward playing an important role in public life was to copy out rules that would tell him how to dress, walk, and eat.

Many of the rules that follow are outlandish in their details, and it would be wrong to drain the fun out of reading them. But they were meant seriously. Maybe they can work on us in the 1990s as the Jesuits intended them to work in the 1590s—indirectly—by putting us in a more ambitious frame of mind.

A Note on the Text

I have modernized the punctuation, and most of the spelling. Gaps in Washington's manuscript have been filled in with the analogous passages from Hawkins's rules, which I have modernized to the language of the eighteenth century.

The Rules of Civility

&

Decent Behavior

In Company

and Conversation

1 Every action done in company ought to be done
with some sign of respect to those that are present.

2 When in company, put not your hands to any part
of the body not usually discovered.

A rule often flouted by rap singers, and pitchers.

3 Show nothing to your friend that may affright him.

Probably this means wounds or dead bodies (see rule #62). There were plenty of occasions in the eighteenth century when such sights would be unavoidable. No need to seek them out.

4 In the presence of others, sing not to yourself with a humming noise or drum with your fingers or feet.

Don't carry a boom box either.

5 If you cough, sneeze, sigh, or yawn, do it not loud but privately; and speak not in your yawning, but put your handkerchief or hand before your face and turn aside.

Lieutenant Colonel Washington, age 22,
facing his first defeat in a frontier skirmish

6   Sleep not when others speak, sit not when others stand, speak not when you should hold your peace, walk not on when others stop.

Before you can tell whether others are speaking, standing, or stopping, you must be aware of them first.

7   Put not off your clothes in the presence of others, nor go out of your chamber half drest.

Still relevant advice for in-line skaters, and other narcissists.

8   At play and at fire it's good manners to give place to the last comer, and affect not to speak louder than ordinary.

"Play" here means cards (as an adult, Washington occasionally gambled, usually at moments of high political tension).

9 Spit not into the fire, nor stoop low before it, neither put your hands into the flames to warm them, nor set your feet upon the fire, especially if there be meat before it.

Today we have stoves and central heat. But the basic point—don't monopolize amenities, or spoil them for others—remains valid.

10 When you sit down, keep your feet firm and even, without putting one on the other or crossing them.

11 Shift not yourself in sight of others nor gnaw your nails.

12 Shake not your head, feet, or legs, roll not the eyes, lift not one eyebrow higher than the other, wry not the mouth, and bedew no man's face with your spittle by approaching too near him when you speak.

Washington, wrote an acquaintance in October 1775, "has so much martial dignity in his deportment that you would distinguish him to be a general and a soldier from among ten thousand people. There is not a king in Europe that would not look like a valet de chambre by his side." See also rules 14, 18, 37, and 76.

13 Kill no vermin, as fleas, lice, ticks, &c., in the sight of others. If you see any filth or thick spittle put your foot dexterously upon it, if it be upon the clothes of your companions put it off privately, and if it be upon your own clothes return thanks to him who puts it off.

Useful advice on the frontier. In 1748, when Washington was sixteen, he went surveying in the Blue Ridge mountains and was obliged to sleep under "one thread bare blanket with double its weight of vermin." The last two clauses are useful anywhere: Don't embarrass those you help, and however embarrassed you may be to discover that you have been in a ludicrous or disgusting situation, don't forget to thank those who helped you out of it.

14 Turn not your back to others, especially in speaking. Jog not the table or desk on which another reads or writes. Lean not upon anyone.

15 Keep your nails clean and short, also your hands and teeth clean, yet without showing any great concern for them.

The modification is as important as the rule. Fussing about your appearance can be as bad as slovenliness. See also rules 52 and 54.

16 Do not puff up the cheeks, loll not out the tongue with the hands or beard, thrust [not] out the lips or bite them, or keep the lips too open or too close.

The mention of beards shows how old-fashioned the Rules were when Washington copied them—by the mid-eighteenth century, men had been shaving their faces clean for more than a generation—though beards have made several comebacks since.

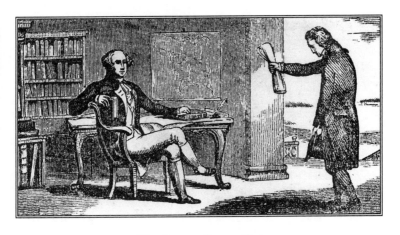

Washington learns that
he has been elected President

17 Be no flatterer, neither play with any that delight
not to be played withal.

*In 1757, during the French and Indian War, the
young Washington, then a colonel in the Virginia
militia, wrote the British commander in chief in North
America, pressing a military scheme upon him. "Do
not think, my Lord, that I am going to flatter;
notwithstanding I have exalted sentiments of your
Lordship's character and respect your rank, it is not
my intention to adulate. My nature is open and
honest and free from guile!" Rule #17 was evidently
hard to learn.*

Celebrating a British victory
in the French and Indian War

18 Read no letters, books, or papers in company, but when there is a necessity for the doing of it you must ask leave. Come not near the books or writings of another so as to read them unless desired, or give your opinion of them unasked. Also look not nigh when another is writing a letter.

Leon Trotsky used to read books at meetings of the Soviet Politburo when he felt his comrades were behaving stupidly (which he often did). No doubt this disposed them to approve of his assassination.

19 Let your countenance be pleasant but in serious matters somewhat grave.

Recent presidents have lost the knack of the "somewhat grave" countenance—they give sickly little grins or turn up shining eyes.

Washington did weep after a farewell dinner with about twenty officers at Fraunces Tavern in New York, December 4, 1783, at the end of the Revolutionary War. In a strained voice, he toasted them—may "your latter days . . . be as prosperous and happy as your former ones have been glorious and honorable"—then asked "if each of you will come and take me by the hand." General Henry Knox, commander of his artillery, embraced him instead. "In the same affectionate manner," wrote one who was there, "every officer in the room . . . kissed and parted with his general in chief. Such a scene of sorrow and weeping I had never before witnessed."

But this was after eight and a half years of danger and privation, and victory against immense odds. Now public figures choke up at the drop of a hat.

20 The gestures of the body must be suited to the discourse you are upon.

21 Reproach none for the infirmities of nature, nor delight to put them that have in mind thereof.

A modern corollary might be to urge those with infirmities to be moderate in making public displays of them to advance favorite causes. Sometimes the gesture can be appropriate. But modern political conventions, which have become veritable processions of the lame and the halt, have clearly carried the practice too far.

22 Shew not yourself glad at the misfortune of
another though he were your enemy.

*The emphasis in this rule, and the next, is on the
show rather than the feeling. But we can infer that
magnanimous thoughts may be inspired by
magnanimous comportment.*

23 When you see a crime punished, you may be
inwardly pleased, but always shew pity to the
suffering offender.

24 Do not laugh too loud or too much at any public
spectacle.

*Washington attended plays whenever he could, both
tragedies and comedies. He was observed to laugh in
the theater only once—during his presidency, at a mild
joke at his own expense.*

25 Superfluous compliments and all affectation of
ceremony are to be avoided, yet where due they
are not to be neglected.

*"Affectation"—ceremony for its own sake, or to show
that you are being ceremonious—is bad. The rituals
that follow are matters of custom and marks of respect,
not ends in themselves.*

26 In pulling off your hat to persons of distinction,
[such] as noblemen, justices, churchmen, &c.,
make a reverence, bowing more or less according
to the custom of the better bred, and quality of
the persons. Among your equals expect not
always that they should begin with you first, but
to pull off the hat when there is no need is
affectation. In the manner of saluting and
resaluting, in a word, keep to the most usual
custom.

*Washington prepares to give his
step-grandaughter, Nelly Custis, in marriage*

27 'Tis ill manners to bid one more eminent than yourself be covered, as well as not to do it to whom it is due. Likewise he that makes too much haste to put on his hat does not well, yet he ought to put it on at the first, or at most the second time of being ask'd. Now what is herein spoken, of qualification in behaviour in saluting, ought also to be observed in taking of place and sitting down, for ceremonies without bounds are troublesome.

Don't tell someone who is more important than you are—a boss, perhaps, or a host—to dispense with a ceremony. But if you are asked not to bother, don't bother.

28 If any one come to speak to you while you are sitting stand up, though he be your inferior, and when you present seats, let it be to everyone according to his degree.

29 When you meet with one of greater quality than yourself, stop and retire, especially if it be at a door or any straight place, to give way for him to pass.

30 In walking the highest place in most countries seems to be on the right hand, therefore place yourself on the left of him whom you desire to honour. But if three walk together the middest place is the most honourable. The wall is usually given to the most worthy if two walk together.

31 If anyone far surpasses others, either in age, estate, or merit, yet would give place to a meaner than himself, the one ought not to accept it. So he on the other part should not use much earnestness nor offer it above once or twice.

32 To one that is your equal, or not much inferior,
you are to give the chief place in your lodging
and he to who 'tis offered ought at the first to
refuse it, but at the second to accept though not
without acknowledging his own unworthiness.

*This rule became Washington's model for politics as
well as hospitality. He accepted all the great offices he
ever held with reluctance and modesty. When the
Continental Congress chose him to be Commander in
Chief in 1775, he told them. "I do not think myself
equal to the command I am honored with." When he
was elected to preside over the Constitutional
Convention in 1787, he "lamented his want of better
qualifications, and claimed the indulgence" of the
delegates "towards the involuntary errors which his
inexperience might occasion." In his first inaugural
address in 1789, he declared himself "peculiarly
conscious of his own deficiencies." Many rulers make a
show of modesty, of course, including tyrants. But
Washington, from long practice, meant it.*

The Constitutional Convention,
Philadelphia, 1787

33 They that are in dignity or in office have in all
places precedency, but whilst they are young,
they ought to respect those that are their equals
in birth or other qualities, though they have no
public charge.

Washington demonstrated the first clause of this rule
at the inauguration of John Adams, his successor.
When President Adams finished his inaugural address
and left the podium, Washington and Thomas
Jefferson, the new Vice President, remained behind.
Jefferson held back to let Washington leave next, but
Washington gestured that he must go first: the Father
of his Country would follow the Vice President.

34 It is good manners to prefer them to whom we
speak before ourselves, especially if they be
above us, with whom in no sort we ought to
begin.

The first inauguration,
New York, April 30, 1789

35 Let your discourse with men of business be short
and comprehensive.

*This goes for businessmen, and authors of business
books, too. See also rule #61.*

36 Artificers & persons of low degree ought not to
use many ceremonies to lords or others of high
degree, but respect and highly honor them, and
those of high degree ought to treat them with
affability and courtesy, without arrogancy.

*Years after the Revolutionary War, an old veteran
remembered that Washington rode up to his unit to
inspect the landscape with a field glass. The young
soldier asked if he could have a look, and the
Commander in Chief, without comment, handed him
the glass. Obviously, if Washington was busy, he would
not have done it, and if the youth had asked rudely,
Washington would have handed him more than a field*

glass. But high-spirited teenage privates did not disconcert him.

How did Washington treat persons of the lowest degree in his society—his slaves? A diplomat's wife noted, during his presidency, that, though Washington had "acquired a uniform command over his passions on public occasions . . . in private and particularly with his servants, its violence sometimes broke out [i.e., he lost his temper with them]." On the other hand, a Polish visitor to Mount Vernon thought that Washington treated his slaves "far more humanely than . . . his fellow citizens of Virginia." Washington performed his most humane act in his will, in which he directed that all his slaves be freed at Martha's death. She freed them in December 1800.

Martha Washington

37 In speaking to men of quality do not lean nor look them full in the face, nor approach too near them. At least keep a full pace from them.

Probably the most famous apocryphal story about Washington, after the cherry tree, claims that Alexander Hamilton, at the Constitutional Convention, bet Gouverneur Morris, a fellow delegate, that if he would go up to Washington, slap him on the shoulder, and say, "My dear general, I am glad to see you looking so well," Hamilton would buy Morris dinner. Morris supposedly won the bet, but said that the stern look Washington gave him was the worst rebuke of his life. It is most unlikely that Hamilton or Morris, civil men both, would have pulled such a stunt, least of all on Washington.

38 In visiting the sick, do not presently play the physician if you be not knowing therein.

39 In writing or speaking, give to every person his due title according to his degree & the custom of the place.

40 Strive not with your superiors in argument, but always submit your judgment to others with modesty.

"Modesty" is a thread that runs through many rules—32, 41, 52, 87. It is the prerequisite for rule #1. Only a man who does not thrust himself forward will be capable of noticing his companions, and judging what signs of respect they are entitled to.

41 Undertake not to teach your equal in the art
himself professes; it savours of arrogancy.

*All his life, Washington was willing to take advice:
from his generals during the war, from James Madison
in the history and designing of constitutions, from
Alexander Hamilton in finance. He also knew when to
stop taking advice, and make the decision.*

42 Let your ceremonies in courtesy be proper to the
dignity of his place with whom you converse, for
it is absurd to act the same with a clown and a
prince.

"Clown" means rustic.

43 Do not express joy before one sick in pain, for that contrary passion will aggravate his misery.

44 When a man does all he can though it succeeds not well blame not him that did it.

When Washington was sixty-seven years old, he went riding in a snowstorm and came down with an acute sore throat. Probably it was a staph or a strep infection, in which case nothing could have been done for him by the medicine of the day. What his doctors did was painful as well as useless—drawing off pints of blood, applying hot plasters. Washington knew he was dying, yet remembered to say: "I thank you for your attentions, but I pray you to take no more trouble about me."

45 Being to advise or reprehend any one, consider whether it ought to be in publick or in private, presently, or at some other time, in what terms to do it; & in reproving shew no sign of choler, but do it with all sweetness and mildness.

A very hard lesson for Washington to absorb, considering his temper. But the only time he berated someone in public was at the Battle of Monmouth Courthouse in 1778, when Charles Lee, one of his generals, had fallen back instead of attacking. Appearing on the scene, Washington asked the reason for the disorder. Lee stammered; Washington did not. At his court-martial, Lee described himself as "disconcerted, astonished, and confounded by the words and the manner" of his Commander in Chief. See also rule #49.

46 Take all admonitions thankfully in what time or
place soever given, but afterwards not being
culpable take a time & place convenient to let
him know it that gave them.

47 Mock not nor jest at any thing of importance,
break no jests that are sharp, biting, and if you
deliver any thing witty and pleasant, abstain from
laughing thereat yourself.

*See also rule #72. We are more likely to jest at
anything, however serious, and to applaud ourselves for
doing so.*

48 Wherein you reprove another be unblameable yourself, for example is more prevalent than precepts.

Washington did not disdain precepts: he copied out all 110 rules by hand, and when he had become an authority figure, he dispensed advice to his younger relations (love, he wrote one of Martha's granddaughters, "ought to be under the guidance of reason") and to colleagues (your "lively and brilliant imagination," he warned an American diplomat, heading for an assignment in Paris, ought to be "under the control of more caution and prudence").

But good behavior is a better teacher than any amount of lectures: a lesson often lost on Americans. Once the lectures were about hard work, now they're about recycling. But the national tropism to cant remains. In our myths we depict ourselves as strong, silent types—cowboys, detectives, sturdy mothers in walk-ups or homesteads. Would that we were.

49 Use no reproachful language against any one, neither curse nor revile.

Some of Washington's earliest general orders as Commander in Chief forbade cursing and swearing. One veteran, describing his loss of temper at Monmouth Courthouse, said he swore "till the leaves shook on the trees." But the soldier who "remembered" this had not actually been present. His "memory" was hearsay, thereby ignoring rule #50.

50 Be not hasty to believe flying reports to the disparagement of any.

51 Wear not your clothes foul, [or] ript, or dusty, but see they be brush'd once every day at least and take heed that you approach not to any uncleanness.

The First Family

52 In your apparel be modest and endeavor to accommodate nature, rather than to procure admiration. Keep to the fashion of your equals, such as are civil and orderly with respect to times and places.

53 Run not in the streets, neither go too slowly nor with mouth open. Go not shaking your arms, kick not the earth with your feet, go not upon the toes, nor in a dancing fashion.

54 Play not the peacock, looking every where about you, to see if you be well deck't, if your shoes fit well, if your stockings sit neatly, and clothes handsomely.

Washington cared deeply about his clothes and how he looked all his life, often designing his own uniforms ("the coat to be faced and cuffed with scarlet and trimmed with silver; a scarlet waistcoat with silver lace; blue breeches; and a silver laced hat"). Did he violate rules 52 and 54? The key is how you behave after you are dressed: do not "play the peacock," or try to "procure admiration."

Posing in an old uniform, 1772,
three years before donning another

55 Eat not in the streets, nor in the house, out of season.

56 Associate yourself with men of good quality if you esteem your own reputation; for 'tis better to be alone than in bad company.

See rule #58.

57 In walking up and down in a house, only with one in company, if he be greater than yourself, at the first give him the right hand and stop not till he does and be not the first that turns, and when you do turn let it be with your face towards him. If he be a man of great quality, walk not with him cheek by jowl but somewhat behind, but yet in such a manner that he may easily speak to you.

The Rules here show their origins in an aristocratic age, when some people held a superior position by virtue of birth. But democracy does not abolish authority—it confers it for stated times, by stated means. Those in authority deserve special marks of respect. See rule #33.

58 Let your conversation be without malice or envy, for 'tis a sign of a tractable and commendable nature, and in all causes of passion permit reason to govern.

This rule, and rule #56, look to externals: ". . . if you esteem your reputation": ". . . 'tis a sign of a tractable and commendable nature." But if you keep good company, and avoid backbiting, even if only to look good, eventually the habits will rub off.

59 Never express anything unbecoming, nor act against the rules moral before your inferiors.

60 Be not immodest in urging your friends to discover a secret.

61 Utter not base and frivolous things among grave and learn'd men, nor very difficult questions or subjects among the ignorant, or things hard to be believed. Stuff not your discourse with sentences among your betters nor equals.

Thomas Jefferson had served with Washington in Virginia's colonial legislature and with Franklin in the Continental Congress. "I never heard either of them speak ten minutes at a time, nor to any but the main point, which was to decide the question. They laid their shoulders to the great points, knowing that the little ones would follow of themselves."

62 Speak not of doleful things in a time of mirth or at the table; speak not of melancholy things as death and wounds, and if others mention them, change if you can the discourse. Tell not your dreams, but to your intimate friend.

Or your psychoanalyst.

George Washington's

favorite indoor sport

63 A man ought not to value himself of his atchievements or rare qualities of wit, much less of his riches, virtue or kindred.

64 Break not a jest where none take pleasure in mirth; laugh not aloud nor at all without occasion; deride no man's misfortune tho' there seem to be some cause.

65 Speak not injurious words neither in jest nor earnest; scoff at none although they give occasion.

If this rule were generally practiced, there would be no studio audiences for daytime TV talk shows.

66 Be not froward but friendly and courteous, the first to salute, hear, and answer. Be not pensive when it's a time to converse.

"Froward" means "stubbornly contrary, obstinate."

67 Detract not from others, neither be excessive in commanding.

Washington wrote a nephew who was about to go into the Virginia legislature, "Never exceed a decent warmth, and submit your opinions with diffidence. A dictatorial Stile, though it may carry conviction, is always accompanied with disgust."

68 Go not thither, where you know not whether you shall be welcome or not. Give not advice without being asked, and when desired do it briefly.

Many of Washington's guests at Mount Vernon ignored rule #68—they showed up uninvited.

69 If two contend together take not the part of either unconstrained, and be not obstinate in your own opinion. In things indifferent be of the major side.

At the Constitutional Convention, Washington changed his vote on a contested point, telling James Madison that "it was not of very material weight with him & was made an essential point with others who if disappointed, might be less cordial in other points of real weight."

The Washingtons entertain Lafayette
at Mount Vernon

70 Reprehend not the imperfections of others for that belongs to parents, masters, and superiors.

71 Gaze not on the marks or blemishes of others and ask not how they came. What you may speak in secret to your friend deliver not before others.

See also rule #21.

72 Speak not in an unknown tongue in company but in your own language and that as those of quality do and not as the vulgar. Sublime matters treat seriously.

"Unknown tongue" also applies to jargon, or the slang of one age group. Don't go on and on about Woodstock to kids, or 'zines to adults.

73 Think before you speak, pronounce not imperfectly, nor bring out your words too hastily, but orderly, distinctly.

74 When another speaks be attentive yourself, and disturb not the audience. If any hesitate in his words, help him not nor prompt him without [being] desired. Interrupt him not, nor answer him till his speech be ended.

Let a speaker complete his own thoughts, even if he is having trouble. If he is having extreme trouble, one might follow the example of the Speaker of the Virginia House of Burgesses when the young Washington, a famous but awkward war hero, found himself unable to talk on his first day as a legislator. "Sit down, Mr. Washington," the Speaker said, "Your modesty equals your valor, and that surpasses the power of any language that I possess."

INDÉPENDENCE

The American hero,
A French view

75 In the midst of discourse ask not of what one treats, but if you perceive any stop because of your coming you may well intreat him to proceed. If a person of quality comes in while you're conversing, it's handsome to repeat what was said before.

If you come into a conversation late, don't expect everyone to backtrack for you. But you may do it for others. The old-fashioned use of the word "handsome" recalls the proverb: "Handsome is as handsome does." At six feet, three and one-half inches, in an age of short people, Washington was an imposing figure—but he was all the more imposing for the way he behaved.

76 While you are talking, point not with your finger at him of whom you discourse, nor approach too near him to whom you talk, especially to his face.

Many of the rules (12, 14, 18, 37) deal with space and distance—"approaching too near," "lean not upon anyone," "look not nigh," "keep a full pace from them." Keeping your distance is a sign of respect, and not keeping it is a sign of disrespect, as so many contemporary metaphors for unseemly behavior show—"in your face," "touchy-feely."

77 Treat with men at fit times about business & whisper not in the company of others.

Don't ring someone up on your cellular phone either.

78 Make no comparisons and if any of the company be commended for any brave act of virtue, commend not another for the same.

79 Be not apt to relate news if you know not the truth thereof. In discoursing of things you have heard name not your author. Always a secret discover not.

One of the few times that Washington spoke at the Constitutional Convention was to upbraid an unknown delegate for leaving his copy of the minutes (which were secret) lying about. "I must entreat Gentlemen to be more careful lest our transactions get into the newspapers. . . . I know not whose paper it is, but there it is, let him who owns it take it." One delegate (not the culprit) noted that no one ever claimed the paper.

80 Be not tedious in discourse or in reading unless you find the company pleased therewith.

81 Be not curious to know the affairs of others, neither approach those that speak in private.

82 Undertake not what you cannot perform but be careful to keep your promise.

When Mary Washington, George's mother, was told of one of his victories during the Revolutionary War, she is supposed to have commented, "George generally carries through anything he undertakes."

83 When you deliver a matter do it without passion & with discretion, however mean the person you do it to.

"Deliver a matter" means convey a message, give an order.

84 When your superiors talk to anybody hearken not, neither speak nor laugh.

85 In company of those of higher quality than yourself, speak not till you are ask'd a question, then stand upright, put off your hat, and answer in few words.

After bidding farewell to his officers at Fraunces Tavern, Washington went on December 23, 1783, to Congress, which was sitting in Annapolis, to surrender his commission—an appearance that Congress had carefully choreographed. He stood while Congress sat. He handed the paper not to the presiding officer, but to an aide. Then he read a brief statement. The protocol had been worked out by Congress to demonstrate its primacy over their wildly popular Commander. Washington agreed totally with the form, and the message; in his mind, Congress was more important. (His diffident behavior made him even more popular, of course.) Washington returned to Mount Vernon on Christmas Eve.

86   In disputes, be not so desirous to overcome as not to give liberty to each one to deliver his opinion and submit to the judgment of the major part, specially if they are judges of the dispute.

Even when Washington himself sat in the role of judge—as Commander in Chief at councils of war or President at meetings of what we now call the cabinet, he expected his subordinates to give their opinions. "Perhaps the strongest feature in his character," wrote Jefferson, "was prudence, never acting until every circumstance, every consideration, was maturely weighed."

87   Let your carriage be such as becomes a man grave, settled, and attentive to that which is spoken. Contradict not at every turn what others say.

88 Be not tedious in discourse, make not many digressions, nor repeat often the same manner of discourse.

89 Speak not evil of the absent for it is unjust.

90 Being set at meat scratch not, neither spit, cough, or blow your nose except there's a necessity for it.

Washington did a lot of entertaining in his life—for friends and strangers at Mount Vernon; for members of Congress, foreign diplomats, and the occasional Indian chief during his presidency. As President, he was sometimes stiff—one guest noticed him playing with a fork, "striking on the edge of the table with it"—for the table was not truly his own. At Mount Vernon, he was more relaxed, and sometimes (in the words of one guest) "sent the bottle about pretty freely." It was good that table manners were well drilled into him, for he was called upon, more than any other American, to make use of them.

91 Make no show of taking great delight in your victuals. Feed not with greediness. Eat your bread with a knife, lean not on the table, neither find fault with what you eat.

"Eat your bread with a knife"—that is, cut it into bite-sized pieces.

92 Take no salt or cut bread with your knife greasy.

93 Entertaining anyone at table it is decent to present him with meat. Undertake not to help others undesired by the master.

94 If you soak bread in the sauce, let it be no more than what you put in your mouth at a time, and blow not your broth at table but stay till [it] cools of itself.

Washington ended dinners by toasting,

"To all our friends."

95 Put not your meat to your mouth with your knife in your hand, neither spit forth the stones of any fruit pie upon a dish nor cast anything under the table.

96 It's unbecoming to stoop much to one's meat. Keep your fingers clean & when foul wipe them on a corner of your table napkin.

97 Put not another bit into your mouth till the former be swallowed. Let not your morsels be too big for the jowls.

98 Drink not nor talk with your mouth full, neither gaze about you while you are drinking.

99 Drink not too leisurely nor yet too hastily.
Before and after drinking wipe your lips.
Breathe not then or ever with too great noise,
for it is uncivil.

100 Cleanse not your teeth with the table cloth
napkin, fork, or knife, but if others do it, let it
be done with a pick tooth.

*Pick tooth means toothpick. If people will clean their
teeth at the table, do it with the smallest implement
possible.*

101 Rinse not your mouth in the presence of
others.

*The point of these last ten rules is ultimately not to
be gluttonous, but first, not to give offense to your
fellow diners.*

102 It is out of use to call upon the company often to eat. Nor need you drink to others every time you drink.

103 In company of your betters be not longer in eating than they are. Lay not your arm but only your hand upon the table.

104 It belongs to the chiefest in company to unfold his napkin and fall to meat first. But he ought then to begin in time & to dispatch with dexterity that the slowest may have time allowed him.

A rule formulated for large dinner parties, when it takes time to serve everyone: Don't start eating until the host does, but the host should start soon to give everyone time to finish. Host and guests attend to each other.

105   Be not angry at table whatever happens & if
you have reason to be so, show it not but [put]
on a cheerful countenance especially if there be
stranger, for good humor makes one dish of
meat a feast.

106   Set not yourself at the upper side of the table,
but if it be your due, or that the master of the
house will have it so. Contend not, lest you
should trouble the company.

107   If others talk at table be attentive but talk not
with meat in your mouth.

108 When you speak of God or His attributes, let it be seriously & with reverence. Honor & obey your natural parents though they be poor.

109 Let your recreations be manful not sinful.

110 Labour to keep alive in your breast that little spark of celestial fire called conscience.

The only open reminder of what has been implicit all along: Petty morals and large morals are linked; there are no great spirits who do not pay attention to both; these little courtesies reflect, as in a pocket mirror, the social and the moral order.

Bibliography

✢

Recent books on George Washington include Paul K. Longmore's *The Invention of George Washington* (Berkeley: 1988), Richard Norton Smith's *Patriarch* (New York: 1993), and Richard Brookhiser's *Founding Father: Rediscovering George Washington* (New York: 1996).

The standard modern biographies are Douglas Southall Freeman's *George Washington* (New York: 1948–1957), and James Thomas Flexner's *George Washington* (Boston: 1965–1972). Washington Irving's *George Washington: A Biography*, edited and abridged by Charles Neider (New York: 1976) is a significant nineteenth-century treatment.

One-volume collections of Washington's important letters and papers have been edited by W. B. Allen (Indianapolis: 1988) and John Rhodehamel (New York: 1997).

George Washington's Rules of Civility and Decent Behavior, edited by Charles Moore (Boston: 1926), explains the origins of the rules in detail, and reproduces them in Washington's own handwriting.